Unsaid Words
Volume 1- Mental Health
By Cassie Moon

Unsaid Words

Copyright © 2024 by Cassie Moon. All rights reserved. No part of this book is to be used or reproduced in any manner without written permission from the author expecting for the use of brief quotation in a book or scholarly journal. This book is about mental health, emotions that comes with heartbreak and domestic violence please seek professional medical advice should you require it.

For anyone who has struggled with their Mental health

Your not alone

Unsaid Words

Book Introduction

Have you struggled or are struggling with your mental health?
Did you know there are thousands of words we keep hidden in our minds.
Because we are too scared to be judged?

These are all silent thoughts on a good or bad day.
Are you ready to hear what I have to say?
All the unsaid words I kept at bay.
I promise at the end you're make sense of your healing your own way.

Unsaid Words

Mental Health

I am the fixer who refuses fix herself,
I am the girl who says you most love yourself.
I say it's ok to not to be okay.
I help where I can so I can put my own traumas away.
Because I too lost people to mental health this way.
Everyone I have ever been around has struggled mentally.
Am I finding them accidentally?
Am I still trying to find my identity?
Am I fixing others so I can give up on myself potentially.
I know I must practice what I preach, but what if I drown as I speak.
Healing them means I'm doing something good,
As mental health is all misunderstood.
I wish I could....
Fix everyone to free the trauma inside of me.
However it's a guarantee I'm actually hurting parts of me.

Today I felt like I lost my way,
hiding away from the world for the twelfth day.
I started to Push all my friends away,
because what they don't see is,
I don't want them to be worried for me.
Why would I want my friends to see the broken mess that's inside of me?
I know they just want what's best for me,
But feeling this way is uncontrollable you see.
So i will message back when the depression lets me be free.

I see the battles you have pulled yourself through.
I know being strong is sometimes the only thing you can do.
I hear the silent cry's at night.
Hand over your mouth kinda cry, because somebody dimmed your light.
I promise it gets easier, just please don't give up your fight.
The strength you have inside you is plain to see.
Don't suffer in silence, so please cry to me.
When your head is so loud, but no sound will come out.
Remember the storm will pass and your get through this battle ground.
There is no one like you and that is true.
I will hold your hand while you figure out this view.

I have fought for everyone to be in my life.
Despite nobody fighting to be in mine.
I have bloody knees from where I begged people to fight for me.
And I know most will agree,
That every time I have helped them,
The rope burn gave me first degrees.
Sometimes I hate the empath in me.

I know today's a hard day.
You probably just want to hide away.
I know the feelings you feel,
So just give yourself time to heal.
One day your get through this hurt that's so real

For years we fought to be seen,
now we're criticised because our minds are not always clean .
We see things in black and white there is no in-between.
"Am I high or am I low?"
Because being just ok is something we don't know.
Staring into a different dimension,
it's called dissociation it's not our intention.
Attention seeking Is the world used for people who don't understand our disorder.
When all we have suffered is trauma.
Depression takes over.
We can't function with the stigma of bpd exposure.
To my fellow borderline reading this,
One day your see that there is way to set the borderline free.
To feel peace and calm like a steady sea,
For you hold the key.
I promise you one day your trauma won't define you like it did me.

When the sun spikes to 28 degrees,
Your wrapped up incase somebody sees.
Scared to unwrap to feel that gentle breeze.
You don't want to be judged by another,
but It's the middle of summer.
please don't let fear make you suffer.
All the battle scars are part of your journey.
I know this doesn't concern me,
But forgive yourself for that you don't want the world to see.

I know sometimes you wish it would of worked,
All The attempts we keep unheard.

I'm telling you the reason why it didn't work.
Your life is deserved, so keep telling your story because your voice needs to be heard in this tiny minded world.

When the world goes silent,
and your mind is starting to become violent.
Remember you have been here before,
pain is never easy especially when one's mind is at war.
When your crying on the floor,
I want you to let go once more.
It's time to let your heart start to restore.
You owe it to yourself to live once more.

I know today your fighting with the mind,
It's doing everything to be unkind.
Your pretty don't let those thoughts win,
Your beautiful don't Listern to those thoughts within.
Your body is beautiful.
I know sometimes it makes you tearful.
But i think you're the prettiest best friend I ever had.
I get insecure to so I understand.

I know today's a hard day.
You probably just want to hide away.
I know the feelings you feel,
So just give yourself time to heal.
One day your get through this hurt that's so real

I know you're suffering today.
your screaming for someone to take this pain away,
The darkness keeps pulling you back.
Just take it hour by hour,
if that's what will help you get back on track.
Feel what you need to feel
but don't let pain stop you shining again.
As Sadness is apart of learning to heal.

Hope is what's needed,
When you're torn down from life's experiences.
Heal from the pain, that tortures your brain
Be kind to yourself while you find you again.
You will blossom in time my friend.

As I stared at her reflection, I saw her lose many years to the wrong direction.
The path she took was never always right,
but no matter how much was thrown her way
She never gave up her fight.
At times she wanted to end it all, the pain she endured always made her feel small.
Little does this girl know she always rose and stood tall.
she broke out of the mould that would freeze her soul Ice cold.
To stand there brave and bold,
with a smile on her face as she unfolded the story which was untold.
because the world needed the girl in the mirror
It may have taken years but I finally she her clearer.
I am the unhealed version of the girl in the mirror
but after it all I forgive her

Winter is my favourite season,
I can make up excuses not to leave house,
like blaming the weather that's the reason.
I can feel the cold from the inside, within the four walls I can just hide.
Where nobody can see me cry,
A Feeling of sadness is no lie.
For these are the months where i die a little but promise i do try.
It's -3 degrees or am I falling to my knees?
I have mental health but is it actually a disease?
Count to 10 this feeling will ease.
It's ok to freeze just take it day by day, your no expertise.
Winter is my best reason, because I can truly feel this season.

When did I lose myself so easily,
I didn't even know it was happening.
As I put my make up on I realised I lost my confidence.
The only words I speak of myself is hatred towards my incompetence.
How did I have so much light within me,
when now all I see is the darkness taking over quickly.
I Lost my sanity,
because I allowed people to ruin my reality.
I let the hands of those who hurt,
dismantle every moral I had to protect self worth.
I lost ability to love myself,
I know somewhere somehow I withheld on giving love solely to one's self.
I was to busy pouring all the parts of me,
hoping someone would see the beauty within me.
Who am I staring at in the mirror?
This is not me.
For the girl inside me is fighting to be free.
I'm starting to reconsider,
that I need to give back the love to me that I would deliver.

Before you take your own life,
As I know that's what you want to do,
will you read this letter I wrote dedicated to you.
I know you have probably started to write your own goodbyes,
So that your loved ones will know why.
I urge you to listen because I want to change your mind's provisions.
I want to remind you of all that you are,
so least if you choose listern
you could slightly change your own path from this decision.
Has anyone told you that the world needs more kind hearted souls like you,
You're unique and beautiful but I know your sadness is making you blue.
I beg you to stay,
For as long as it takes just say one more day,
I'm proud of you in every single way,
Promise me that you will stay and keep saying
"One more day"

Is that a smile I see?
I'm finally getting to see the real me.
Who finally gave up letting the pain control my sparkle within me.
I'm going to shine bright,
Because I was made to live this life

She came in for support with her borderline personality disorder.
I saw her stood there and I was in the same corner.
Someone who understood the importance of staying,
Instead of begging as a character we kept role playing.
No longer fighting to be seen,
we are the same there is no in-between.
Little does she know she mended me in my darkest scene.
Healed me until my thoughts run clean.
She listened to my heart break,
Knowing I cried to not wake.
She made it her mission to mend the heartache.
Crying and laughing with me,
Because she knew I needed to heal and be free.
She comes in the form of my best Friend,
One person who never made me question
 "when it would end"
A girl who's Loyal and honest.
She's my best friend,
The girl who did everything with pure intentions,
I would attend hell with you
just to make sure I'm there in the end.

Dedicated to my borderline best friend
Tia Toussaint

I could see the sadness in your eyes,
you're always fed with the worst goodbyes.
Here you are putting on the best disguise,
because you have to find the strength to improvise.
Change is never easy,
I have faith in you so wipe them tears immediately.
Take as long as you need,
To write up that I love me deed.
Then it's agreed,
one more tear in this chapter to set yourself free.

Please know you are not alone
I feel mental health quite deep aswell.
This is another year from hell,
but the smile hides it so well.

I'm scared of living a happy life,
what if it's everything I don't like.
I am scared to love again
so deeply and getting hurt so easily.
Anxiety riddles me ever so freely.
Maybe one day I won't let it over take me constantly.

The pains so bad it hurts when I breathe.
My hearts shattered underneath.
I don't think I have enough strength.
My mind is constantly leading me down the path of death.
Dark I know but it's how my mind is truly feeling.
I can't cope with all the hate Iev been appealing.
I never thought someone who loved me
would team up with the enemy and
 make jokes and lies about my identity.
Knowing it would destroy me mentally.
The pills keep calling me,
And I'm sick of faking I'm ok constantly.
Being strong is all I can do,
I know i will get passed these sad days soon.
But I will never forget the worst days in June.

Another day masking with a disguise.
So that I don't have to answer with ""I'm fine."
I hide it so well most days,
but in my head I feel like running away.

This is on honour of all domestic Violence Survivors

The living and the dead your all still fighters.
Have you ever been afraid to speak?
Knowing that someone you loved would make you weak.
Weak in the worst possible way,
With all the hurtful things they would say.
Emotional abuse is a tactical skill,
Physical abuse gives them a frill.
Mental abuse so they can't be labelled as the one who kills.
Above it all It's your blood that spills.
Every punch or kick silences you not to get out quick.
Did you know it takes up to 12 times to leave?
I been there I know your staying hoping it's love your receive.
A racing heartbeat scared by those foot steps coming towards you,
They don't love you - they love to beat you black and blue.
This is something nobody should have to go through.
I stand with you, as a survivor it's true.
Many of us have been in the same boat as you.
You are never alone, so please don't stay until you're only left with a gravestuone.

Do you ever go silent because words simply don't work anymore.
You don't react you just stare and question humanity, like your a prisoner in capacity.

Borderline gave me a attachment disorder.
So how do I leave when it's nothing but torture?
They don't teach you how to detach.
Only how to keep one relationship in tact.
I guess my vulnerabilities will always be a facility for people to use my liabilities.

I prefer the night time.
When it's 2 am and the sky is dark,
but you can see the stars align.
There's something so peaceful about the night time.
I've spent many nights in dark places when my mental health has declined,
however tonight's not that kind of night.
I have pulled myself out of some dark tunnels and that's how I know that not every night is a bad night.
Tonight my mind is calm and it doesn't mean me any harm.
So if your facing these kind of struggles,
I promise the more you face life,
you will pull through all of your troubles.

I play out scenarios in my head.
Even as a child, I would imagine being dead.
This time I was rushed into hospital and I'm laying in an intensive care bed.
I'm imagining all the people rushing to see me.
The kind words on their own would set me free.
I guess to play scenarios out loud as an adult,
Shows I just wanted to be loved as a child.

If you had a deep conversation with me,
you would know that all I've been doing is fighting to be free.
A conversation like this will take hours because I wasn't born with superhero powers
I was diagnosed with borderline personality disorder.
I wouldn't wish it on anyone because a life with borderline is torture.
I only hold traumatised baggage,
because the little girl inside me carries nothing but damage.

Do you struggle to ask for help?
I know it's hard asking for help with your mental health.
Take some of your strength,
please reach out to somebody and go in depth.
Because you deserve to live and not fantasise about your death.

I think if my heart could bleed out,
There would be multiple buckets spilling over without a doubt.
The hurt inside me is like a story that keeps playing over and over again,
When will this heartbreak end?
I walked away but the pain wishes to stay.
I know I have to now heal the parts of me,
Because it's time I break the chain and set myself free.
For my heart deserves love so purely.

Sometimes I think people wonder why I don't leave.
Trust me I've tried but I also know what it's like to grieve.
It's all the sympathy cards you constantly receive.
The denial that they're gone because you're in disbelief.
The months where everything is at a standstill,
because you still don't understand why somebody would leave you.
I know this feeling through and through,
so please don't leave people who love you.

A poem for the person who is going to love me.
I may not be the easiest to deal with.
If your the person who can heal my heart, then I'll call the locksmith.
At times I will be manic,
and in my depression stages please don't panic.
you need to be thick skinned,
because moods change like the wind.
I will make mistakes and sabotage you to leave.
when in fact I just want you to stay and that's something I've never received.
My head and my heart battle to believe,
that anyone could love borderline me.

Unsaid Words

Volume 2 Coming Soon

The author Cassie Moon

I released this book to help someone else who may be going through a rough patch in their mental health.
I have had many struggles mentally, and I just wanted to share some inspiration as I know what it is like to suffer in silence.
please reach out to professionals if you need support.
Your story needs to be heard.
Don't give up!

TikTok Account - poetrybycassie

Cassie moon

Printed in Great Britain
by Amazon